Dr. Fredrick J. Harris
Presents

WITHOUT LIMITS SCHOOL OF APOSTOLIC &
PROPHETIC MINISTRY
STUDENT ANTHOLOGY EDITION

LION OF JUDAH

Without Limits School of Apostolic and Prophetic Ministry:
Student Anthology

Without Limits Ministries Copyright© 2021

Published by:
EMPOWER ME BOOKS, INC.
A Subsidiary of Empower Me Enterprises, Inc.

ISBN: 978-1954418035

Printed in the United States of America

WITHOUT LIMITS SCHOOL OF *APOSTOLIC* &
PROPHETIC MINISTRY
STUDENT ANTHOLOGY EDITION

Greetings Beloved!

We are dedicated to training & mentoring prophetic vessels for the kingdom assignment within their regions, using practical tools and biblical principles to accurately and adequately operate and exercise the spiritual gifts from an apostolic prophetic realm.

WLMI educates individuals that range from the spiritually immature to the spiritually mature leaders fortified to serve in God's Kingdom. We are honored to serve Abba, Father, in the loving leading and instruction of His children. We are here to serve your spiritual, educational needs for such a time as this.

No longer shall you perish from lack of knowledge. Wisdom and revelation given by the Holy Spirit is vital to the health of your life. "Beloved, I pray that in every way you may succeed and prosper and be in good health [physically], just as [I know] your soul prospers [spiritually]." III John 1:2 AMP. This book was written inspired by the voices of our students and the teachings of our Founders.

Apostle Dr. Fredrick J. & Lady Lakendra Harris

Prophetic Training & Mentoring Academy

Purpose and Vision Statement

PURPOSE STATEMENT

This training academy aims for individuals with prophetic gifts to understand and demonstrate their anointing for kingdom advancement. We are mandated to build the prophet's ministry so that lives will be restored and rejuvenate to continue the fight for righteousness. We decree and declare
Isaiah 55:33 *"incline your ear, and come unto me; hear, and your soul shall live."*

Many believers died and never found their purpose in God's kingdom. A generation of souls perished because of the lack of leadership and instruction. This generation wasn't instructed or led into spiritual birth of destiny or precise aspiration. They have dreams and visions and are navigating in a prophetic atmosphere, to be able to speak the oracles of God to the people.

Prophetic training allows comprehensive understanding to bring forth revelation and move from stagnation to domination. You are destined to reign through prophetic insight, training, and teaching. Your life as a prophet of God is unlike any other because God chose YOU as His servant.

Nothing happens until the prophet **SPEAKS (Supernatural Prophetic Empowerment Advancing Kingdom Servants into Service) Joel 2:21-23.**

VISION STATEMENT

The primary function of the training academy is to educate and demonstrate the gift of prophecy through music, teaching, training, and illustration. We are consecrated to build the ministry of the prophets as it is declared in the Word of the Lord from **Amos 3:7 KJV *"surely the Lord God will do nothing, but he revealeth his secret unto his servants the prophets."***

The prophetic training & mentoring academy is comprehensive and infused with a purpose to teach how to develop, enhance, discern, breath, live, speak and proclaim all dynamics of prophetic ministry. Under the fathering anointing and guidance of an apostle who is a servant of Jesus Christ and utilizing wisdom and compassion for the prophets of God, the secret plans are revealed by the Holy Spirit.

We as believers of Christ Jesus stand firm as pure vessels to decree and declare **Ephesians 3:5 *"which in other ages was not made known unto the sons of men, as it is now revealed unto his holy apostles and prophets by the Spirit."***

This academy is here to train, implement and activate the prophetic gift to the local church and the individual. When all of the *Gifts of the Spirit* are encompassed, we will experience a supernatural lifestyle through apostolic and prophetic ministry.

The Apostolic Council

The Company of Apostles help to train and implement an apostolic dimension that will transform lives to receive signs, miracles, and wonders. In addition, one can overcome demonic opposition and obstacles through the apostolic grace given by the Lord, Jesus Christ, to His people. Without Limits Ministries council brings wisdom, clarity, and insight to the believers and imparts revelation concerning their gifts to function in an apostolic ministry.

LEADERSHIP

Apostles Roger & Jamessica Joyner
TMB Ministry, San Antonio, TX

Apostle Lye & Prophetess Darlene Taylor
Healing Waters Deliverance Ministry, Jacksonville, NC

Apostle Dr. Randy Sr. & Lady Stacey Bell
Zoe Life Ministries, Marietta, GA

Chief Apostle Dr. Ron & Pastor Laverne Spears
Faith & Power Christian Center, Dunn, NC

Apostle Bobby D. & Lady Shiniqua Jordan
True Deliverance Ministries International, Fayetteville, NC

Apostle Dr. Temaki & Mr. Robert Carr
Loving the Nations Missions Ministry, Fredericksburg, VA

"It takes great leadership to resurrect your purpose."
- Chief Apostle Dr. Fredrick J. Harris

The Company of Prophets

LEADERSHIP

ɸ Prophet Denzel Martin
   Fort Campbell, KY

ɸ Prophetess Mother Denise Giles
   Clarksville, TN

ɸ Prophetess Dr. Monique Rodgers
   Raleigh, NC

ɸ Prophetess Fama Fall
   Jacksonville, FL

ɸ Prophetess Lashonda Lackey
   Greensboro, NC

ɸ Prophetess Tamara Huff
   Raleigh, NC

ɸ Prophetess Myrina Robinson
   Durham, NC

ɸ Prophetess Kathie Robinson
   Raleigh, NC

ɸ Prophetess Evangelist Belinda Guyton
   Fayetteville, NC

CERTIFICATION PROGRAMS

Prophetic Ministry Certification
I Corinthians 12; Ephesians 4

School of The Prophets is a comprehensive study into the apostolic and prophetic knowledge of scripture. Within this program, Dr. Harris teaches the fundamentals of God's word and how to apply it as an Apostle, Prophet, Teacher, Evangelist, Pastor, Seer, Intercessor, Dreamer, Warrior, Helper, Administrator, or Administrator just simply as a kingdom citizen. Dr. Harris wrote the in-depth curriculum and training manuals for the program himself.

The School of the Prophets challenges the believers' current mindset and understanding of scriptural knowledge for growth. STP activates through the demonstration of God-given gifts imparted to each of us from the Holy Spirit. This program is rigorous. This program is educational. This program will elevate your walk, relationship, and knowledge of God. Graduates from STP operate at total capacity within the five-fold apostolic ministry, marketplace ministries, local assemblies, and communities. Each graduate gains wisdom, understanding, practical tools, and newfound power and authority with humility to walk in their purpose boldly.

Apostolic Ministry Certification
Ephesians 4:11

There is an apostolic reformation and restoration that has come upon us in this hour. The apostolic and prophetic movements are being established throughout the world for the resuscitation and edification of the church.

This apostolic study is comprehensive and strategic. The benefit is to empower you to complete a task. The anointing from God is for service and does excellent work and stimulates change to the Believer's mindset.

The Apostolic Ministry Biblical Study program was written and created by Dr. Harris and is taught by the Apostolic Council. There is a need for understanding in the body of Christ of what true Apostles are and what exactly is an Apostolic Ministry. This program will elevate your faith, wisdom, revelation, and knowledge of God and the calling upon your life.

Ministry of Administration
I Corinthians 12:28

This certification program will aid in the understanding of adequately utilizing the *Gift of Helps and Administration* as defined in I Corinthians 12:28 within the local body of believers. The Apostle Paul explicitly wrote the importance of unity within the body of Christ for the edification of the kingdom through various gifts administered by the Spirit of the Lord.

"There are diversities of gifts, but the same Spirit. There are differences of ministries, but the same Lord. And there are

diversities of activities, but it is the same God who works all in all. But the manifestation of the Spirit is given to each one for the profit of all" - I Corinthians 12:4-7

The Spiritual *Gift of Helps and Administration* is a unique God-given ability to plan, organize, support, and define order within a ministry and organization. People with this gift ensure the success of an assignment from God by implementing the strategies given through prophetic visions. Lady Lakendra has written and created this program to impart how to be an effective administrator and support your local assembly. The desire is that you are ignited to see the value of yourself in the gift God has given unto thee.

Life Coach Certification

Without Limits Ministries offers Life Coach training for congregations, ministry leaders, and individuals.

In this specialized training, Dr. Harris, a certified Christian Life Coach through Freedom Bible College, provides professional & spiritual coaching to implement strategies and plans for enhancing success through biblical life applications to remain focused and resilient in a complex society.

The Life Coach Certification Course is offered through distance learning virtually. It's a highly interactive online biblical foundation course. This course is available in three different stages:

1. Beginners - Three-day course
2. Advanced - Two-day course
3. Refresher - One-day course

DEDICATION

Topics in this book are not meant to be a syllabus or a complete regurgitation of the content taught. Instead, it is rather useful inspired apostolic and prophetic principles taught or gained by the students and instructors throughout the courses over time. This book is dedicated to the Student Writings of Without Limits Ministries International.

Apostle Dr. Temaki Carr
Apostle Lyle Taylor
Apostle Bobby Jordan
Apostle Dr. David R. Watkins
Elder Toney White
Elder Damaris Bostic
Evangelist Laura Finley
Evangelist Evelyn Streets
First Lady Sharonda Armour
First Lady Tonya Watkins
Minister Bessie McDaniel
Minister KaSonya Miller
Minister Twanda McIver
Pastor Dr. Raymond Bell
Prophetess Darlene Taylor
Prophetess Mary Quick
Prophetess Tamara Huff
Prophetess Belinda Guyton
Prophetess Dr. Monique Rodgers
Prophetess Kathie Robinson
Prophet Denzel Martin
Prophetess Fama Fall
Prophetess Lashonda Lackey

Prophetess Pamela D. Williams
Pastor Debbie Rios—Merritt
Pastor Sonia Yanez
Pastor Frances Perry
Prophetess Tracey Hairston
Prophetess Mary Stratford
Pastor Trisha Waters
Prophetess Tammye Holt
Prophet Ernest McIver
Prophet Brian Stewart
Prophetess Chosen Boston
Prophetess Dolores Jones
Pastor Howard Merritt
Prophetess Nakeida Prescod
Sister Mercedes Toney
Sister Tanya Egelston
Sister Aisha Gates Harris
Sister Jessica AA Highsmith

CONTENTS

....

Apostolic & Prophetic

INSPIRATIONS, GOVENANCE, TEACHINGS & LESSONS LEARNED

LION OF JUDAH

TOPIC 1: LAYING THE FOUNDATION FOR LOVING THE WORD OF GOD.

One student reflects, "There is an importance in being identified by God. We are all here in the darkness, but unless he calls us and we answer, we are still bound to darkness like all the others. Once he stands knocking at your door, and you open it up, he gives us the responsibility to learn of him. How do we do this by first confessing with your mouth the Lord Jesus and believe in thine heart that God raised Him from the dead thou shall be saved? Then through getting in the word of God, praying, and asking to be filled. We often think we don't need the Holy Spirit, but if you want to learn the Truth, you have to have it so that you can receive the revelation that's in the word of God.

If we just read the Bible, it will be like just reading a story, but when you read the Bible and study it and meditate on it through prayer and the Holy Ghost, you will understand the mysteries revealed. Once you have received the understanding and lead and guide the Holy Spirit, the Lord will begin to talk to you and give you instructions that you will have to follow. This is the beginning of your first assignment to learn of him and except, him as your Lord and Savior Jesus Christ.

I accepted the Lord three times in my lifetime. The first time was when I was about nine; I wanted a new white dress and coming up Baptist; I always thought there was more. Then again, when I was a teenager, I understood more about what it meant to be saved. Growing up in a single-parent home, the church played a big part in my life because I was a girl, and my mom wouldn't allow me to stay home with my brothers. She always made arrangements for me to be in summer camp or vacation bible study or somewhere doing something with the church. I learned a lot about how the church is run, but I also saw a lot that made me pull away.

Then when I was an adult in Fort Polk standing in my kitchen, I heard the Lord call my name. I asked my husband if he was calling me he said no, so after the third, Tracey, I said, " Here am I speak, Lord. He said, today is the day you go back to church. So, in 1992 I answered the call and went to Agape Church of God and Christ under Pastor Ronald Jones. From there, I was taught the basics and had to eat the whole scroll. I was introduced to the Holiness denomination, for the word says without Holiness, no man shall see the Lord. But when God calls us to be Holy, it should be our lifestyle, not just a denomination."

As a leader, we can impact lives significantly, and sometimes we only get one chance, so we must be sound and practical to make a difference. Our role as a leader is to help create a desire in others to become better, even when sometimes we cannot feel God's presence. Psalms 139 says that God's spirit is wherever we are; therefore, we are never without him. Everyone wants to know that someone cares about them and when you can meet the need of a person or people, you are creating a path that leads to trust. God has a purpose for each of our lives, and he trusts us to carry out his plan. When we surrendered our lives to Christ, we became God's Child or a co-heir to Jesus. We belong to him, and no one can take that away. We have entered into a faith covenant because of God's love which is given freely to us. We are required to share it with others.

Prayer is the first line of defense in any plan or strategy for living out the principles of God. It will help if you become successful in creating an environment for change to take place. As we gather together, the power of unity and prayer sets a standard for others to follow. Each leader has different life experiences to bring to the table that we can meet each person on common ground. Transparency is an important quality to develop in your leaders because no one is perfect. When we share our stories, others will see that God is all about giving life to those who choose the way through Jesus that he is offering. The disciples asked Jesus to teach

3

them how to pray, and this lets us know that we don't know what to pray sometimes—admitting that this allows you to become free from praying in your own strength and the Holy Spirit is given the space he needs to intercede on our behalf carrying all the burdens.

As a prophet, we are called to be a great example of God's saving grace as he set the standard, and there is no room for compromise. As we use our gifts, we become a great asset in motivating believers and an opportunity to be light to the unbelievers. The *Gifts of God* are without repentance.

Not everyone is called to lead in the ministry of God; they are called to be a leader in their personal lives, and to do that properly, they need prophets to hear and release the Rhema word of God. The Holy Spirit searches all things, even the deep things of God according to I Corinthians 2:10, and the Holy Spirit comes and reveals it to the Prophets to help the people of God to divide the word of God rightly. We see a lot of Christians going to church hearing the word and can quote the word of God, but when you ask them how the text applies to their lives, they cannot tell you. They received the letter of the word, but not the spirit of the word, which brings life and clarity to their circumstances and issues in their homes, market places, and the church.

Prophets cannot afford to get entrapped in their emotions because people need prophetic strength. Prophets must be able to confront the darkness and use their prophetic authority. The prophet's heavenly language, speaking in unknown tounges, is vital when facing dark forces. The Holy Spirit guide lives. Prophets are concerned about the affairs of people. The Prophetic realm helps people to come to God in a wholesome manner. This is the season prophets must teach people to surrender their lives to God.

TOPIC 2: HOW TO ENCOUNTER THE ART OF PROPHETIC MINISTRY; IS TRAINING NECESSARY?

A prophet is a foreteller of future events, a predictor, a person illuminated or inspired by God to announce or communicate the heart and oracles of God in the earth. Acts 13 describes the Church at Antioch, which was described by Merriam – Webster of 1828 as a school or college in which young men were educated and qualified for public teaching. These students were called "Sons of the Prophets." Many often question the need for schools or apostolic or prophetic training. The Holy Spirit indeed trains all prophets through inspired revelation; however, to be sound for the times and cultures that we live in. This is to ensure we understand how to gracefully flow in the mantle or sphere of influence that God has called us to, requires us to seek training to sharpen the gifts so that we may operate in full capacity once called upon. Remember Joseph. His Father trained and equipped him, even though he knew that God had graced him prophetically. Samuel was being prepared for years without knowing he was being taught, and when he proved mature in spirit, God called out to him.

There are five levels of prophecy which include:

1. The Manifestation of Prophecy. This is when a prophetic word is spoken, and the word comes to the past. Not necessarily that day or even the next day, but whenever God allows that word to come to past.

2. Gift of Prophecy. Is the Spirit given the ability to receive and communicate timely spirit-inspired messages from God.

3. The Grace of Prophecy, is the grace given to use the Gift

of Prophecy correctly and in a timely matter. If you are misusing the Gift of Prophecy, not to the glorification of the Lord, the gift will be there, but God removes his Spirit, and then you aren't effective. Think about King Saul.

4. Spirit of Prophecy- When Prophets come together and are operating under the Spirit together, healing revelation and knowledge come forth.

5. Office of Prophecy is a specific ministry stemming from someone's life story and who has been chosen by God to help correct and point the church back to God.

Two groups of the prophets' mantle are *Executive* and *Administrative.* If you genuinely want to learn more, you *must* sign up for this class.

To know their prophetic purpose, you must seek wisdom, knowledge, understanding, and have a clear mind and a pure heart to bring a prophetic message from God to all. Use your gift of prophecy to intercede in the pulling down of strongholds. If you desire to be a free-flowing vessel that hears clearly and a vessel that does not get haughty or begins to slow down because they seem to be overlooked or disregarded, then you are ready to encounter your prophetic purpose. It's time to rise and become the mighty vessels that can push past childhood traumas and cast down imaginations or thoughts of being less than qualified; it's time to press forward. Your purpose is to do the will of God and to serve in the kingdom, and remain humble, ready, and willing.

Only God knows what needs to be accomplished, and He is the only One qualified to complete that work in and through you. Through each prophetic purpose, God has ordained you and called you to be effective and impactful in His kingdom! He has sent you to proclaim the gospel that the captives will be released, that the blind will see, and that the oppressed will be set free. You are called to the masses in some form or another; whether called a Staff Prophet, a Resident Prophet, a House Prophet, a Shamar Prophet, a Sanctuary Prophet, an Apostle, a Teacher, a Pastor, an Evangelist, or as the prophet over your home. Remember, you are a servant First, and you are called to serve and build, build and then equip.

Training provides direction, a plan of action, clarity, a spiritual Kiosk of sorts for strategy, and even healing and deliverance.

TOPIC 3: TEAM BUILDING CONCEPTS FOR APOSTLES AND PROPHETS

A prophet speaks a word from God that will exhort God by turning his people towards Him. A prophet is to comfort God's people by encouraging word from God and is to edify and strengthen the body of Christ. The prophet sometimes has to give a word of correction for the body to stay in alignment with God's will for his people. The prophet might have a word for the corporate ministry or an individual to build up the church. Let's examine an example of a Prophet and Teacher team co-laboring in ministry.

A teacher in the church plays a vital part in growing and learning in your faith. You can read the Bible on your own or go to church on Sunday mornings and hear a preached word from the pastor, a topic with a few pinpoints with little detail. It takes you going to Sunday School, Bible Study, or any other small group led by a teacher who has the knowledge of the Word that can break down the scripture to your understanding that allows you to apply it in your lifestyle.   The teacher will give opportunities to answer questions that you need to further your understanding and knowledge. A teacher can teach in a corporate setting in church or conferences or individual studies at home or over the phone. The teacher teaches to build up the church.

The significance of the prophet and the teacher co-laboring together in covenant team ministry is that when the Body of Christ comes together in corporate ministry, they are to edify the Body of Christ in agreement. For example, the prophet would go forth with a word from God that will pertain to details on specific steps you will have to make during a coming time in your life. The teacher will instruct you with the Word of God from his written instrct6ions in the Bible. Psalm 119:105 says that the Lord's word is a lamp for my feet, a light on my path. The taught word will sustain your way until the manifestation of the prophecy.

When the prophet and teacher work together in their perspective area, the word that the prophet spoke not only will come to the past but with the instruction of the teacher, you are destined to stay in God's will according to God's plan. Imagine just how the prophet and apostle pair with other five-fold gifts; it truly takes the ENTIRE body of gifts!

TOPIC 4: WORKING IN THE CORPORATE ANOINTING WITH A PROPHETIC PRESBYTERY AND RECEIVING THE PROPHETIC SPIRIT OF THE LEADER

Did you know that prophets are agents? They are Ambassadors, Consuls, Delegates, and Intermediaries. Prophetic companies and ministries should work hand in hand together for unity within the body. As a prophet, the prophecy is delivered in parts. Each prophet is responsible for the delivery of their part. There should be unity in the delivery, revelation, and impartation. Working together is essential. Within the five-fold ministry, it is critical to know what area you are operating within the apostolic realm. As signified in Ephesian 4:11, each office is vital for a church to thrive. If you are operating in Apostolic/Prophet going to a church where an Apostle is preaching or delivering a message, then your role wouldn't be to serve as an Apostle at that moment. Instead, you would operate as a prophet, as long as the Apostle welcomes you in that role. It is essential to make sure that you are in alignment and operating in a place of order.

We must prophetically have the spirit of our leader, who should embody the heart of God. Deuteronomy 1:9-13 states, "At that time I said to you, "You are too heavy a burden for me to carry alone. The LORD your God has increased your numbers so that today you are as numerous as the stars in the sky. May the LORD, the God of your ancestors, increase you a thousand times and bless you as he has promised! But how can I bear your problems and your burdens and your disputes all by myself? Choose some wise, understanding and respected men from each of your tribes, and I will set them over you." We must move from stagnation and formulate a team to grow where God wants us to grow. Get with God and do your best. Be prayerful and quiet before God. Be a God –Investor.

When God establishes a principle, it is to be for advancement within his economy. The economy is synonymous with government. He has to host and develop an environment to build in. It is within this environment that he has given his people great responsibility. The passage in Ephesians states instances of the gifts given for the building of his mandates. His prophetic economy thereby brings enrichment of knowledge and revelation to the kingdom. Economies are significant, which exemplify kingdom mandates. The spiritual benefits for advancement get pillars of glory in his economy; thus, spiritual realms must be invaded. The church and Body of Christ are elevated in their position and can operate with this enhancement for the work of the ministry (Ephesians 4:11-12).

For instance, in the book of Nehemiah, this is an excellent example of a fortified prophetic foundation working. Nehemiah states," the God of heaven will prosper us; therefore we his servants will arise and build." Once God spoke to him, he knew that nobody was greater; nor had a right to keep him from his homeland in Jerusalem. He saw his enemies as irrelevant in their taunting. Their threats were a waste; Nehemiah already had a permissible plan in place from the King, most notably Gods' approval. Unbeknownst to the government officials, namely Sanballat and Tobiah. Nehemiah had his prophetic clearance already sanctioned. He was not coming in to build by himself. His servitude to the King gained him favor. The authority he brandished made the Samaritans uneasy, even angry. Nehemiah utilized strategic stealth strategies to keep his plans from disruption. Even the Jewish leaders did not know the whole matter. Yet his rebuilding blueprint is in heaven and shortly will be on earth (Neh.2:4, 17-19, Matthew 6:10).

The fulfilled prophecies of Zechariah and Daniel are necessary for this economy. Daniel is taken into captivity, yet he still is used mightily. He knows that God is faithful as well as sovereign. The Prophetic Foundation was set with the plans already spoken and now being manifested for all the nations and people to see. Daniel states, "Now listen and understand! Seven sets of seven plus, sixty-two sets of seven...., Jerusalem will be rebuilt, with streets and strong defenses, despite the perilous times" (Daniel 9:25 NLT).

Psalm 51 depicts God's love and faithful help. The contrast of David and Nehemiah both needing confidence that can only come from God. The desire for David denoting the net that they had prepared for him. Likewise, Nehemiah knew his soul was among lions, and their tongues were sharp swords. In verse 4, grief overtook Nehemiah. With intent, he had to trust his heart to God. He knowingly contemplated that God must be merciful unto him; as he wept to see the destruction of the wall and his people, the Jews (Neh. 1:4).

Indignantly, the people were enduring hardships, harassment, and even bondages. But the good news was that the angel was moving swiftly to assist God in his promise to return his people. He states that "God was still jealous for Jerusalem and Zion with a great jealousy" (Zech. 1:11-14).

Zechariah and many other prophets tended to blend their prophetic foundations into panoramas. They understood that there was an eternal God who would establish an eternal Kingdom. They all knew that He would conquer his enemies and strengthened the people. The prophets knew this one thing; hope is found in God and his Messiah, who rules over the entire earth.

God is a fortress whose assignments are strategic. He has shown his fortified wonders and shall subdue the people under us. He is in total control of the world. **(**Psalm 47:1-2; Psalm 91:12).

TOPIC 5: APOSTOLIC STRATEGIES THAT IMPACT INFLUENCE, AND MANIFEST MIRACLES

Suppose one had to solve a problem in the apostolic decision-making process; the apostolic training manual serves as an excellent guide. On page 54, it states the three most essential things in our lives. They are the Holy Spirit, our kingdom assignment, and our seed.

Through every fleshy decision made off of gut instinct vs the knowledge inspired by the Holy Spirit, you must learn the importance of consistency in studying and meditating on the word of God and prayer. God's grace and mercy cover our mistakes, as Holy Spirit is the teacher of what is right and what is just. We must learn to speak to the Lord concerning *all* things!

God can send the strategy through prophetic dreams, symbols, and prophetic understandings. We must stand firm and receive the strategy and be unmovable from what He has given unless He tells us our next move. Checkmate!

If you are a dreamer or seer and need help understanding and interpreting your dreams, then you should attend the Prophetic Dream Academy at WLMI.

Numbers 12:6: "When there is a prophet among you, I, the LORD, reveal myself to them in visions, I speak to them in dreams." Jeremiah 33: 3: "Call to me and I will answer you and tell you great and unsearchable things you do not know."

As prophetic leaders, we must embrace the struggles, confusion, spiritual warfare, and past victories. Wrestling with the prophetic call amid battling traditionalism has been preparatory. Sometimes our most significant spiritual deficiency or battle is allowing the apostolic flow to engulf our lives honestly. To possess what God has for you requires your complete attention/focus on the divine.

Just like the Army, we need to be able to analyze and assess the situation. As apostolic and prophetic vessels, we must not be blind to what is happening in the realms around us. Territorial spirits are lurking and running amuck. We are called to have dominion and influence Jesus' name where we occupy. The mission may call for a specific strategy or auspice to operate within. But if we are blindsided and caught off guard, we may get more than what we bargained for!

We must be able to conduct ourselves in such a way that God's righteousness will flow directly through us. His spirit must rise through our earthen vessels to accomplish the mission. We were taking strategic steps with each course of action. God has sent us to be the change. Not to go in and be changed. At least not in a negative aspect, that is. Victory should be established with each decision we roll with. God knows what we were made for and capable of. We get sent because we are the representatives and ambassadors delegated to operate in his name.

So, in conclusion, we would solve problems by ushering in the Holy Spirit. By inviting the presence of God, decreasing our own understanding of a matter, and completely surrendering to Him. I would seek that clarity and knowledge of the matter that I am being called to solve problems strategically—never be blind or off-kilter, as I like to say—using the Apostolic decision-making process to my advantage. And not thinking or believing I can do it on my own, in nothing but my flesh and worldly understanding.

Furthermore, we must be intentional in following God's directives according to his word and the spirit's function. Being disciplined in this spiritual posture will launch my confidence and release your prophetic/apostolic giftings to a greater heavenly dimension.

TOPIC 6: THE DYNAMICS OF PROPHETIC MARRIAGES

If we were to design the family team for the nation and church according to Hebrews 10, then we would be a family of believers where everyone is known and loved. Regardless of where we have come from, we are a family in Christ. When we all operate in forgiveness, hope, faith, and love, we can all head in the same direction growing in God's image unified. Families could then engage with God and allow for Him to strengthen them. His purpose and destiny for the families will be restored to serve emerging nations and generations jointly. Marriages would be how God constituted them as a lifelong commitment between a man and a woman at the beginning of creation. After all, Marriage was the first ministry instituted by God.

When God calls our marriages, we have been chosen to leave a legacy. The legacy of how our body operates and functions will be the key to generational curses being broken. When we allow God to lead and guide us in building, it will bring clarity and God perfected understanding. Our body is not our own and does not belong to us. As a family unit, our body or union belongs to Christ.

Be sure to Check out the WLMI Marriage Seminars!

TOPIC 7: DISCERNING THE LAWS OF THINKING

The Bible says, "For you are all children of God through faith in Jesus Christ. It is as if you have put on new clothes when we have been baptized and united with Christ (Gal 3:26 NLT).

The people who feel that they are not equipped to receive the Lord's blessings are not looking at God, but instead, they are looking at their reflection. God said from the beginning that he made man in His image and His likeness (Genesis 1:26). These people must decide to forego the lifestyles of their flesh which represents sinful nature. When man continues to go their independent thinking, utilizing their personal framework as a reference, it locks God out. This mannerism will become a vexation of the flesh and the spirit. For even the Apostle Paul struggled within. He stated," for that which do not allow; for what I would that I do not." He continues in this discontentment as he attempts to deal with his old nature (Romans 7:15, KJV).

Whether it be sin, disbelief, or even having an un-regenerated spirit, it has to be disciplined. These feelings of vulnerability are dealt with through mentorship, leadership, and sacrifice to begin a life of Christian growth. People must take a spiritual approach of realization, of having the Father's seal. This requires prayer, then activation of Jesus as the Son of God.

The realm of stretching their faith will take courage, coupled with sound bible reading and teaching. They were applying principles of the lessons learned to assist in expanding their expectations. Faith requires prayer, fasting, and even being quiet: to ask God for interpretations of His spectacular life. They must accept the benefits of what God has already done. When they see some colors or events that stand out brightly, be assured to denote God. Seeing orange is a way that the Holy Spirit is attempting to get their attention for a change. This change is subtle and can even consist of a warning.

This warning can be a faith move to come out from self-imposed character traits of disbelief. Faith must overrule the fragile mind, leading the people to overcome their fears. Believing Jesus and taking him at his word is crucial. The people who believe have to commit this very fact. Because the Word of God is the Truth of God, he and His word are synonymous. The word of God is quick, sharp, and it is alive. Everyone knows that a bear has physical strength. The Word of God gives spiritual strength.

The strength to interpret His will revokes indecisiveness. It gives way to listening and actions of faith. Relying on faith requires hearing the Word of God. The activating of those senses allows for seeing as well. An indicator of movement in the spirit realm gives way for opportunities to draw nearer to God. For example, colors can become invitations of restoration. The color white, for instance, the people must respond to this. They then wonder: is God saying surrender, thus making more confident decisions for Him (Heb. 4:12, Romans 10:17). In the book of John, Jesus says that God has sealed in and all that he is. This being said, everlasting life is through the Father and His son Jesus. People cannot waver at the signs or rituals of spiritual life. They must keep believing in an everlasting life that endures.

Jesus was named the Beloved Son, Bread of Life, and Son of God because he fulfilled all righteousness. People have to make choices that reflect the sanctification process. Fruitful lives are directed by Holiness and an everlasting life in Jesus. They have to put those feelings aside and accept that they are free from sin. They have to lay aside every weight of neutrality (John 6:27, Mk 1:11, Matt. 3:17).

According to Chapters 7 & 8 in the Prophetic Spiritual Warfare Manual, many people give way to the *spirit of anxiety* and are looking for ways to satisfy the flesh.

After reviewing chapters 8 & 7 specifically, the information about loneliness and depression is certainly an eye-opening reality. The statement particularly pricked the author: it is unfair for people who have the Holy Spirit living inside them to say they are lonely. Having never really thought about that reality, it says that the person is not allowing the Holy Spirit to have free reign in them. They are not fully surrendered to the One who created the universe and themselves. Therefore, they live in a world that is not real. They are living a reality that only exists in their mind. That is so dangerous because scripture tells us that as a man thinketh, so is he.

One minute, they are praising their Lord with their lips, and the next, they are operating as if they have been abandoned by the very God they proclaim. Double-minded...unstable, and therefore should not expect anything from God, because in essence, they do not even know what they believe. So, likewise, they are faithless and spiritually schizophrenic. Understanding that these peoples' loyalty is divided between God and the world allows us to understand why some who are giving way to the *spirit of anxiety* seek ways to satisfy the flesh.

TOPIC 8: DEFINING THE MOMENT
THAT YOU HEARD GOD

Defining the moment you heard God is amazing, but when he uses your hands, it is unique and humbling at the same time. After reading the different types of prophetic classes, one student determined that in the Metron, their prophetic sphere of influence was in Healthcare. The Gift of Healing accompanies the student's Prophetic mantle. A prophet like this is someone who has insight into the needs and functions of the human body. Their anointing gives them revelation into certain illnesses and causes.

They reflected that the first time they thought God had used them to heal was about four years ago. Read their testimony:

"My sister had a pitbull named Gator. They had him for years, and he was a very strong and muscular dog. I was always at my sister's house, so I interacted with the dog a lot. There were times that I would be sitting on the steps on her porch, and he would come and put his face in front of me, and we would lock our eyes into each other, and it seemed like he could see right through me. One day he got sick. He had lost a lot of weight. So much that we could see his ribs through his skin, he had been ill for about a week, and everyone thought he was going to die. One night I walked outside where he was; I placed my hand on his forehead and began to pray.

Now, keep in mind that I was nowhere where I am right now with my walk with the Lord. I was still pretty new to it. But I had faith, and I knew that God could heal because I have actually seen him raise someone from the dead. (but that's a different story) Anyway, I placed my hand on his forehead, closed my eyes, and I began to pray and asked God to heal this dog. Gator was loved, and he was like family, so I asked God to heal him. When I woke up, I walked outside to check on him, and it was as if he was never sick. He was still really skinny, but he was jumping and really hungry. I stood there in amazement and looked up, and I remember asking God, Did you really heal this dog? Did you really hear my prayer? I knew in my heart that he had. I never told anyone about the night I prayed for him. I figured no one would believe me. It didn't matter, though, because Gator was healed. Now I think that was the first time God showed me how he was going to use me. Going back to the time I witnessed God bringing my Pastor's wife back from the dead, I realized that I had to be there that day to see the power of God and what He could do with my own eyes. So when I pray for others, I know it is no for me, but Him who heals, and I am just a vessel. The only downfall is that after I pray for someone, I always get sick. It is scary when I pray for someone, and their spirit latches on to me. But I am learning how to bind anything that comes against me."

REVELATIONS, PRAYERS & STRATEGY

LION OF JUDAH

Prayers

Father, I pray that you reveal clarity and divine revelation to each leader over the North Carolina region. I pray for each person who walks in the prophetic mantel that you will endow an eagle eye in them; An eagle eye that they will see beyond any harm or stranger that tries to interfere or danger, harm, or sickness this our community. I pray that you bind every lying spirit on jobs and interactions to make wealth or take care of our families/friends.

Father, according to your word, Psalms 55:9, confuse the mind of the enemy pray for each neighbor and you will empower and strengthen them with knowledge and understanding how to work together, cover and protect each other wisdom of how to protect their homes.

Father, for our community, you provide strategic strategies for providing education classes and materials to help many in how to repair and create home/business appliances, how to purchase and prepare to eat healthy food, and savings. I pray that you increase each entrepreneur and business with wisdom on assisting and making wealth to increase the need for our communities. Write a strategy & prayer for revelation and strength that would empower your Community troubled by spiritual warfare.

Father, I thank and praise you for my family. Father, I pray for their strength. I pray for encouraging their spirit when they feel hopeless and less confident to endure the assignment or plan you gave them. Father, I pray for salvation in each one of their lives. Especially those who have to backslide. I pray that they will acknowledge their ways and return to you.

I command, declare, and decree the dreams and visions that you have to bestow in them won't die, but that they will awaken and move forward in making it come alive.

I pray that you will fulfill their life that it may balance with their soul (walk with you). Breakthrough believers – are passionate in their pursuit of God and His purposes. There is an intensity about them that matches the "zeal that consumed the Lord Jesus." (John 2:17).

I pray that I will continue to be a light (example) to my family and encouraging them through your word according to Corinthians 10:4, "For the weapons of our warfare are not carnal, but mighty through God to the pulling down of strongholds." You will put true godly (Christian) people in their pathway that will minister to them also coincide with what was already planted in them. Father, I cast down every rebellion, haughty, discord, and jealous spirit within the workplace. I command these spirits to be consumed. I pray according to Colossians 3:24 that you enter in peace, teamwork/player, love, kindness, and loyalty. Father, this pray, command, declare, and decree according to Luke 1:37 "for with God nothing shall be impossible," in Jesus' Name Amen.

Prayer To Awaken To Mature Economics And Dividends

Father God in the Mighty Name of Jesus. We Thank You for this day. We thank You for life, health, and strength. It is in You that we live, move, and have our very being, and without You, we could do nothing, but we can do all things through Christ, who gives us strength. Father, You said in your word that when we pray according to Your will, You hear us, and knowing that You hear us, we know that we have the request we ask of You. Your word also tells me that the fervent effectual prayers of the righteous avails much. It makes power available that is dynamic in it is working.

Now, Father, I know that I am Your workmanship, created in Christ Jesus for good works, which You have prepared for me beforehand, that I should walk in them. Help me to walk in those good works that You have already prepare for me, that I may walk in them. I declare that I will walk in the things that You have called me to do. When I feel inadequate or unsure of myself, help to know that I can do all things through Christ that gives me strength. I understand that the Greater One lives in me. I do not have to lean to my own understanding, and I do not have to go in my own strength.

In all my ways, I acknowledge You, and You direct my path. This Father will enable me not to spend time on things that I should not be caught up in. I yield myself to the power of the Holy Spirit. I shed the spirit of false burden today, and I walk in God's perfect will. Walk with me and talk with me. Go with me and go before me and lead me in the path of righteousness for Your namesake.

You said in Your word that You would show kindness to anyone You want and mercy to anyone. You want. I receive Your kindness and Your mercy today. When I feel that I am not equipped for Your blessings, remind me that You have equipped me with all that I need to do Your will. You are producing in me, through the power of Jesus Christ, every good thing that is pleasing to You. The blessings of the Lord make rich and adds no sorrow. I thank you that I am walking in the richness and the fullness of Your blessings. Father, I know that when I pray, the weapons I use are not carnal, but they are mighty through You to the pulling down of strongholds. Open my eyes and allow me to see clearly in the spirit. Help me to die daily and to surrender to Your precious Holy Spirit. Help me put on the whole armor so that I can stand against all the enemy's tactics. As I seek Your kingdom and Your righteousness, I know that everything I need will be given to me.

I thank You that that through the power of Christ, that You always cause me to triumph. I receive Your favor upon me and my children for a thousand generations, and my family and their children. Now unto him, that can do exceedingly abundantly above all that I ask or think, according to the power that is working on the inside of me, be all glory and honor, majesty, and power, both now and forever, in Jesus name I pray, amen.

If you have doubt in your mind or feel unsuitable that God can't use you, that is not true. Invest in your mind the Word of God for yourself, and you will know the Truth. You might feel unsuitable. I pray that God restores your mind and spirit. If you want to be born again and you are sincere, God is a forgiving God. Father God, I come to you in the name of Jesus Christ, and I decrease that you will increase. I pray that God keeps you steadfast in all your ways. Like the sky changes colors one time, it is orange, red, blue, or white. As you line yourself up with the Word of God, you will see a transformation in your life. I pray that God gives you strength like a bear-like an elephant weights 300 as a baby, then as they grow 1000. I pray God increases you in abundance in every area of your life. Like the eagle, you are free in Jesus' name, amen.

II Corinthians 5:17, "Therefore if any man is in Christ, he is a new creature: old things are passed away; behold, all things are become new." Live for God, and you will never go wrong.

According to Chapters 7 & 8 in the Prophetic Spiritual Warfare Manual, many people give way to the spirit of anxiety and are looking for ways to satisfy the flesh. This is a prayer to help bring deliverance and change.

Gracious Heavenly Father, we thank, and we praise you for who you are. We thank you that Jesus came to give us life and that more abundantly. We praise you for your word that is a lamp unto our feet and a light unto our pathway. Father God, you told us in your word to be anxious for nothing, but in everything by prayer and supplication, with thanksgiving, we are to let our requests be made known to you; and your peace, which surpasses all understanding, will guard our hearts and minds through Christ Jesus.

So, Lord, according to your words, we stand on your promises and refuse to give in to anxiety, but in all of our ways, in all situations and through all circumstances, we acknowledge you so that you can direct our path. Lord, when the enemy comes in like a flood, we declare that the Holy Spirit shall raise the standard against him. We declare that no weapon formed against us shall prosper and that every tongue that rises up against us in judgment shall be condemned. For this is the heritage of the servants of the Lord, and its righteousness is of you, Father.

Our flesh will not control us but put our flesh to death this day by yielding to your precious Holy Spirit. The enemy's lies will no longer lead us, but we walk in the Truth that Christ has revealed so that we can be made accessible. We will walk in the Spirit and will not fulfill the lusts of our flesh. We reject every spirit that tries to make us feel lonely. We reject the lies and ask you, Lord, to wash us, cleanse and purge us from every spirit that causes us to feel lonely.

We close our ears to the lies of the enemy, and we open our hearts to the Truth of your word. For you have told us that you would never leave us, not forsake us, even to the ends of this earth. Lord, we repent for falling into self-pity, doubt, and fear. If we have been double-minded, we repent. Create in us a clean heart and renew the right spirit within us.

Restore to us the joy of our salvation, and we will be careful to give you all the glory and all the praise, in Jesus' name, Amen.

Prophetic Declarations

Hallelujah! You are to be praised! Blessed is the name of the Lord. You have done great and mighty things for me. You have walked in the shadow of the valley before I even knew who you were.

I am blessed beyond measure to be called your daughter.
You are my strength and my portion, my stronghold in times of trouble you hold me in the weary places.

Your love endures forever; it encapsulates me like my mother's womb.

My heart and my flesh may fail, but you, my God, carry me through the temptation of lust, pride, anger, selfishness, and my weaknesses. I cling to you, my Daddy, in your embrace.
Restore my home stronger than before. Let the peace that surpasses all understanding reign our home. Keep your angel army guarding our coming and going.

Your favor is like ripe berries on the vine of my life. You are my husband, Hallelujah! You are to be praised! Blessed is the name of the Lord. You have done great and mighty things for me. You have walked in the shadow of the valley before I even knew who you were.

I am blessed beyond measure to be called your daughter.

You are my strength and my portion, my stronghold in times of trouble you hold me in the weary places.

Your love endures forever; it encapsulates me like my mother's womb.

My heart and my flesh may fail, but you, my God, carry me through the temptation of lust, pride, anger, selfishness, and my weaknesses. I cling to you, my Daddy, in your embrace.

Restore my home stronger than before. Let the peace that surpasses all understanding reign our home. Keep your angel army guarding our coming and going.

Your favor is like ripe berries on the vine of my life. You are my husband and my boss.

Thank you, Jesus, for erasing the damaging things from our past and helping us go beyond the boundaries of self to your will, your calling, and your kingdom.

I am your masterpiece, your Truth Warrior, unique inspirer, chain breaker. No enemy can stand in my presence because I am positioned exactly where you want me to be. Hallelujah! You are to still be praised! Blessed is the name of the Lord! And my boss.

Thank you, Jesus, for erasing the damaging things from our past and helping us go beyond the boundaries of self to your will, your calling, and your kingdom.
I am your masterpiece, your Truth Warrior, unique inspirer, chain breaker. No enemy can stand in my presence because I am positioned exactly where you want me to be. Hallelujah! You are to

Still, Be Praised! Blessed Is The Name Of The Lord!

Prophetic Decree Over Your Life

I decree and declare that I am fearfully and wonderfully made in the image and likeness of God. I decree and declare that I am an heir of God and a joint heir with Christ. I decree and declare I am predestined, called, justified, and glorified in Christ Jesus. I decree and declare that I have the mind of Christ, and I will always do all things through Jesus Christ, for he strengthens me to do the greater works in the earth. I decree and declare that the weapons of my warfare are not in the flesh but mighty through God to the pulling down of every stronghold and every imagination that attempts to exalt itself above the Truth of Jesus. I decree and declare that I live the abundant life in the power of his Holy Spirit.

I decree and declare that I will always seek the kingdom of God daily to know the instructions, strategies, will, knowledge, and understanding of God's assignment for me every day. I decree and declare I will daily repent and daily forgive as I continue to grow and develop in the knowledge of my Lord and Savior, Jesus Christ. I decree and declare that I will always thirst and hunger for Christ's righteousness, and he will fill me with more of his Holy Spirit. I decree and declare that I will daily submit, surrender, yield, walk humbly, and walk-in his meekness daily. I decree and declare that no weapon that is formed against me shall ever prosper. I decree and declare that I will listen diligently to the voice of the Lord, observe and do all he is commanding me to do daily.

I decree and declare in all of my ways I will acknowledge all of them, and they shall direct my path and lead me in the way of everlasting life. I decree and declare that I will be strong and take courage in the Lord. I decree and declare that I will do all God is calling me to do, and I will not turn to the left nor to the right, but I will walk in the way, the Truth, and the life of Jesus Christ. I decree and declare that I will meditate day and night on the word so that I will produce good fruit and good success.

I decree and declare that I will prosper even as my soul prospers in the Lord. I decree and declare that I will hide the word in my heart that I might not sin against them. I decree and declare that I will not be afraid nor dismayed, for God is with me everywhere I go. I decree and declare that the word of God is a lamp unto my feet and a light unto my path. I decree and declare that now faith is my portion daily. I decree and declare that I walk and live by faith. I decree and declare that I live and walk in the Spirit.

I decree and declare that I will accomplish all that God has purposed me to do for the kingdom of God and his name's sake. I decree and declare I am above and not beneath; I decree and declare I am the head and not the tail; I decree and declare I am blessed going and coming in the name of Jesus. I decree and declare that I will give only Jesus, so help me God through his Holy Spirit. I decree and declare that I have been sanctified, purged, purified, cleansed, and made right for God's divine plan for my life. I decree and declare I am the righteousness of God in Christ Jesus. I decree and declare that I am hidden in Jesus Christ.

I decree and declare that I am teachable in every season of my life. I decree and declare I will not become stagnant, but I will always grow in the Lord from glory to glory and from faith to faith. I decree and declare that the work they have started in me will be completed until the day of Christ's return because I have committed all of myself to them. I decree and declare that I will daily present my body to the Lord as a living sacrifice holy and acceptable unto God, for it is what I owe to them for giving me everything. I decree and declare that I will daily put on the whole armor of God that I will be able to stand against the wiles of the devil. I decree and declare that I wrestle not against flesh and blood but principalities, against powers, against the rulers of the darkness of this world against spiritual wickedness in high places. I overcome the enemy through the Holy Spirit in prayer.

I decree and declare I seek not my own; I will suffer long, I will be kind, I will not envy, I will not be proud, I will not be selfish or irritable, I will not keep a record of wrong done to me. I decree and declare I will never give up, I will rejoice in the Truth, I will bear all things, I will believe all things, I will hope in all things, and I will endure all things with the Holy Spirit's help. I decree and declare I will grow in the grace of learning daily how to walk in God's unconditional love. Amen!!!

Final Thoughts with Apostle & Lady Kendra:

ROMANS 12:9-11 (NIV)

"Love must be sincere. Hate what is evil; cling to what is good. Be devoted to one another in love. Honor one another above yourselves. Never be lacking in zeal, but keep your spiritual fervor, serving the Lord."

Serving the Lord is the most essential gift that He has given you. As the ready writer and prophetic vessel in the earth, you have greatness that is unlocked for purpose. Let the rivers inside your belly overflow with wisdom and prosperity that only comes from God.

There is someone waiting on you to impart the power of God upon their life. As the Ambassador of the Lord, continue to feed His word and revelation to them who will have an ear to hear, a mind to learn and a heart to receive.

Go the distance in your pursuit for the kingdom of God and allow the frequency of heaven to navigate and communicate the abundance from your sphere of influence. God is pleased with your obedience, now live out your dreams and ambitions as all the citizen of the kingdom rejoice with you.

Kingdom Blessings,

Dr. Fredrick & Lady Lakendra Harris

NOTES:

NOTES:

NOTES:

NOTES:

NOTES:

NOTES:

NOTES:

NOTES:

NOTES:

NOTES:

**NOTES**:

NOTES:

NOTES:

NOTES:

NOTES:

NOTES:

NOTES:

NOTES:

NOTES:

NOTES:

NOTES:

NOTES:

NOTES:

NOTES:

NOTES:

NOTES:

NOTES:

NOTES:

NOTES:

NOTES:

NOTES:

NOTES:

NOTES:

NOTES:

NOTES:

NOTES:

NOTES:

NOTES:

NOTES:

NOTES:

NOTES:

NOTES:

NOTES:

NOTES:

NOTES:

NOTES:

NOTES:

NOTES:

NOTES:

NOTES:

NOTES:

NOTES:

NOTES:

NOTES:

100

NOTES:

NOTES:

NOTES:

NOTES:

NOTES:

NOTES:

NOTES:

NOTES:

NOTES:

NOTES:

NOTES:

NOTES:

113

NOTES:

NOTES:

NOTES:

**NOTES**:

NOTES:

NOTES:

NOTES:

NOTES:

NOTES:

NOTES:

NOTES:

NOTES:

NOTES:

NOTES:

NOTES:

NOTES:

NOTES:

SCHOLARSHIP PROGRAM

BY Wlmi.org/events

The Prophetic Training & Mentoring Scholarship Program is for upcoming high school seniors who have a desire to go to college or into any branch of the military service. The PT&M scholarship is awarded yearly at the annual Shoreline Prophetic Conference in Carolina Beach, North Carolina. If you're selected as a recipient, you must be present at the Shoreline Prophetic Conference in order to receive the scholarship. Failure to show will result in your disqualification.

The PT&M scholarship was established to celebrate and support the youth of today in their continued educational development and goals as a young adult.

Scholarship Requirements:
1. Current High School Senior
2. Graduating GPA of at least 3.0 of higher
3. 15 hours of community service (waved for COVID)
4. Essay of at least 500 words explaining what will be your contribution to society and the kingdom of God after graduating college.

For questions pertaining to the scholarship program contact withoutlimitsministries@wlmi.org or visit www.wlmi.org/academy

Upcoming & Weekly Events

BY Wlmi.org/events

We strive to provide comprehensive scriptural foundations with life applications through teaching, mentoring and training by the leading of the Holy Spirit. We're happy to serve the people of God weekly through our conference line.

Daily Prayer
Monday - Friday 6 A.M. EST - 33 Minutes of Prayer & Exhortation
Call in at (720) 650-3030 access code 572020#

Weekly Teachings by the Company of Prophets
Every week you can join us by dialing:
(415) 464-6800 access code 10012006#.

- Tuesday 7 P.M. EST - The Prophet's Chamber
- Thursday 7 P.M. EST - Apostolic Joy Night
- Saturday 8 A.M. EST - Supernatural Saturday
- 4th Mondays 7 P.M. EST - She Has Something to Say (Pastor's Round Table)

Monthly Teachings by Chief Apostle Dr. Harris
- 2nd Sundays - Freedom & Fire Radio/TV Broadcast (Available on Facebook Live or view on Star Cable Channel 16 or listen on radio WLCN 1170AM)
- 4th Fridays - 7 A.M. EST - Financial Fire Friday

Annual Events

- **Shoreline Prophetic Conference**
  Wlmi.org/shoreline

  Get ready to receive imparation, revelation and insight through dynamic teaching! Conference is filled with opportunity for Baptism, Fellowship and Ordination for applicable candidates. Held Yearly in Wilimington Beach, NC.

- **Life Coach Refresher Training**
  Wlmi.org/events

  Christian Life Coaches are fundamentally equipped through scriptural truths thast will help them to coach people into a better quality of life and establish goals for purpose.

- **Virtual Prophetic Infusion Seminar**
  Wlmi.org/events

  Join us LIVE on Zoom with Dr. Fredrick J. Harris and Apostle Enoch Owusu Sekyere for activation and empowerment of the Lord's people for the greater purpose of their kingdom assignments. The apostolic grace and prophetic insight will be strategically established for the manifestation of signs, miracles, and wonders.
  Zoom ID: 865-351-2230
  Password: NewLife

- **Apostolic Roundtable**
  Wlmi.org/events

- **Women's Empowerment**
  Wlmi.org/events

- ➢ **Virtual Prophetic Marriage Seminar**
  Wlmi.org/events

- ➢ **Business & Entrepreneur Seminar**
  Wlmi.org/events

- ➢ **Prophetic Book Club Virtual Seminar**
  Wlmi.org/events

- ➢ **Virtual Prophetic Dinner Experience**
  Wlmi.org/events

- ➢ **Prophetic Bootcamp Virtual Seminar**
  Wlmi.org/events

ABOUT THE FOUNDERS

There is a heart for teaching and loving God's people at Without Limits Ministries.

WLMI, an Apostolic & Prophetic Ministry was founded October 1, 2006.

This ministry has a responsibility & accountability to produce sons & daughters in the gospel of Jesus Christ.

Although known for building the ministry of the prophet, WLMI embarks on helping the Believer in developing a closer relationship with the Lord Jesus Christ.

Through the Holy Spirit, WLMI encourages and develops Kingdom Builders through the ministry of reconciliation, peace, and order.

This purpose is for winning souls for Christ while empowering both generations now and to come. Dr. Harris and Lady Harris have formulated many tools which are implemented throughout conferences, seminars, services to provide comprehensive and strategic developmental tools for the end time remnant church.

For Speaking Opportunities, or Bio and Speaker Sheets, they can be obtained at https://www.wlmi.org/ministry-bios-info

OTHER TITLES BY WLMI
TRAINING & MENTORING ACADEMY

Prophetic Training & Mentoring Academy:
Course Study Training Manual
ISBN: 979-8603032-77-1

Prophetic Dream Atmospheres & Spiritual Climates: *Training Manual*
ISBN: 979-8603413-06-8

Engaging in Spiritual Warfare Training Manual
ISBN: 979-8604434-89-5

Made in the USA
Columbia, SC
09 July 2021